A · LITTLE

Chicago Cookbook

Judith Ferguson

ILLUSTRATED BY
SUSAN DAVID

First published in 1994 by
The Appletree Press Ltd
19–21 Alfred Street
Belfast BT2 8DL
Tel. +44 232 243074 Fax +44 232 246756
Copyright © 1994 The Appletree Press, Ltd.
Printed in the E.C. All rights reserved.
No part of this publication may be reproduced or
transmitted in any form or by any means, electronic or
mechanical, photocopying, recording or any information
and retrieval system, without permission in writing from
The Appletree Press Ltd.

A Little Chicago Cookbook

First published in the United States in 1994 by
Chronicle Books, 275 Fifth Street,
San Francisco, CA 94013

ISBN 0-8118-0645-6

9 8 7 6 5 4 3 2 1

Introduction

Chicago. The city was named after its river, and the river took its name from the Native American word for "wild onions" which grew along its banks. The city expanded in a way those first inhabitants would never have imagined. Carl Sandburg, a native Chicago poet, called his hometown the "city of big shoulders". I've always liked to think he meant that Chicago was big enough for everyone. At one time or another, this city on the shores of Lake Michigan has been home to many of the nationalities of the world, which has lead to a lot of diversity, both cultural and culinary.

Every type of food you can think of you'll find in Chicago's kitchens: Eastern European, Irish, Italian, German, Asian, Mexican food; the list just goes on and on. You can pick up a quick sandwich or sit down to haute cuisine. You'll find everything from chic "big city" food to grandma's favorite recipes.

When I think about the city of my birth, certain foods always come to mind: my grandmother's cabbage rolls and chicken soup, Marshall Fields Walnut Room's Sandwich, and chocomint pie – a Chicago favorite.

Mention Chicago, and gangsters come to mind, but there is more to the city than pinstripes and violin cases. From the South Side to the North Shore, from the lakefront to the west side, people are cooking up their old traditions and creating new ones. In fact, each summer the city celebrates with an enormous food festival, so everyone can taste a little bit of Chicago. There's a little bit of Chicago in this book, too.

Chicken Spaetzle Soup

When the winter wind blows off the lake, a steaming bowl of soup with tender chicken and German-style dumplings is just the thing to warm you up!

---

2 lb cut-up chicken
1 bayleaf
1 carrot
1 celery stick
$^1\!/_2$ onion
salt and pepper
1 large egg, beaten
$^3\!/_4$ cup all-purpose flour
$^1\!/_4$ cup water
pinch of salt
1 tbsp chopped parsley
(serves 6)

Place chicken in a large pot with bay leaf, carrot, celery, and onion. Add water to cover, a pinch of salt and pepper, and bring to a boil. Partially cover and simmer about 1 $^1\!/_2$ hours or until chicken is very tender. Strain and reserve stock. Discard vegetables and bayleaf. Remove skin and bones and cut chicken into bite-size pieces. Skim fat from the stock and return to the pot along with the chicken. Mix egg, flour, water, salt, and parsley together. Add more flour or water as necessary to make a very thick paste. Spread paste on a plate. Bring the soup to simmering. Cut spaetzle mixture into short strips about $^1\!/_4$-inch thick and drop them into the soup. Simmer until dumplings float to the surface. Serve hot.

Cheddar Chowder

A favorite quick lunch for busy Michigan Avenue shoppers, this is a velvety cheese soup with celery, carrots, and clams.

---

4 tbsps margarine
4 tbsps each chopped onion, carrot, and celery
4 tbsps all-purpose flour
6 1/4 cups milk
2 large potatoes, diced
1 pt shelled small clams
2 cups shredded sharp Cheddar cheese
salt and pepper
(serves 4–6)

Melt the margarine in a large pan and cook the onion, carrot, and celery until softened, but not brown. Stir in the flour and gradually add the milk. Add the potatoes and bring to a boil. Partially cover and simmer gently, for 20 to 25 minutes, stirring frequently. When the potatoes are almost tender, add the clams and cheese. Cook gently until clams and potato are tender and cheese is melted and smooth. Serve immediately with croutons or oyster crackers.

Wild Rice Soup

A creamy soup that really accents wild rice, yet also stretches that delicacy a bit further. It's a rich first course, so serve small portions.

$^1\!/_2$ cup wild rice
4 strips of bacon, diced
1 small onion, finely chopped
3 sticks of celery, finely chopped
1 clove of garlic, crushed
4 cups chicken stock
1 cup cream
2 tbsp cornstarch
2 tsps Worcestershire sauce
salt and pepper
chopped fresh chives
(serves 6)

Rinse rice well and drain dry. In a skillet cook bacon slowly until golden brown. Remove and set aside. Discard all but 2 tablespoons of the bacon fat. Add onion, celery, and garlic and cook slowly until softened. Remove from skillet, put in a large saucepan, add rice and stock and bring to a boil. Simmer about 1 hour or until rice is tender. Add more stock or water as the soup cooks, if needed. Mix cream and cornstarch and stir into the soup. Bring to a boil, stirring constantly until thickened. Add Worcestershire sauce and bacon and season to taste. Serve with croutons and sprinkled with chopped chives.

Dilled Salmon Terrine

A stylish first course which can be prepared one day in advance. This recipes serves 8–10 people but can easily be halved.

---

1 1/2 lbs salmon, filleted and skinned
1/2 lb sole fillets, skinned
3 eggs
2 cups heavy cream
2 tbsps chopped fresh dill
3 drops of Tabasco sauce
pinch of salt and white pepper
4 oz smoked salmon, diced
mayonnaise
red salmon caviar
sprigs of dill to garnish
(serves 8–10)

Heat oven to 350°F. Chop salmon and sole finely by hand or blend or process thoroughly. Separate eggs and add 2 yolks and 3 whites and process or mix thoroughly until well blended. Fold in cream, dill, Tabasco, and seasoning. Lightly oil a 12 x 3 x 4 inch loaf pan or terrine. Spoon in a layer of salmon mixture and scatter over diced smoked salmon. Repeat with remaining salmon mixture and smoked salmon. Cover with greased foil and place terrine or loaf pan in a pan of warm water about 1-inch deep. Bake for 45 minutes to 1 hour or until a skewer comes out clean. Weigh down the top with a heavy pan or plate and chill until firm. Slice and serve garnished with mayonnaise, caviar, and sprigs of dill.

Shrimp de Jonghe

A first course that is not for the cholesterol conscious! However, half-fat butter substitutes work equally well, and so do other shellfish.

---

1 stick butter
2 cloves of garlic, crushed
1/2 cup dry breadcrumbs
1 lb raw, peeled shrimp
1/2 tsp chopped tarragon
1 tbsp chopped parsley
pinch of nutmeg
1/4 cup fish or vegetable stock
4 tbsps dry sherry
1 tbsp lemon juice
salt and pepper

Heat oven to 400°F. Melt butter in a medium skillet and add garlic. Cook slowly, about 2 minutes. Mix half of the garlic butter with the dry breadcrumbs and set aside. Add the shrimp to the rest of the butter and cook slowly until just turning pink. Add herbs, nutmeg, stock, lemon juice, and salt and pepper to taste. Spoon mixture into 4 ungreased ramekins and add sherry to each. Top with buttered breadcrumbs and bake uncovered for about 10 minutes. Serve hot.

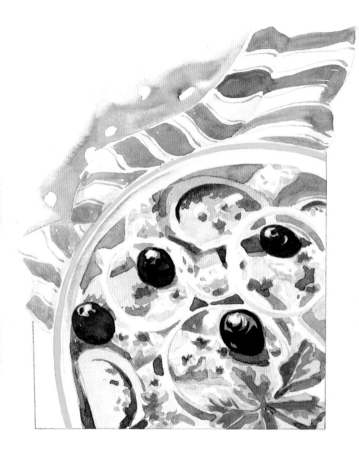

Greek Salads

A cookbook on Chicago food would not be complete without a Greek recipe or two. These salads are among the best.

Greek Taverna Salad

2 beefsteak tomatoes
$^1/_2$ red onion, thinly sliced
1 green or yellow pepper, deseeded and thinly sliced
$^1/_2$ cucumber, thinly sliced
16 black olives

1 cup crumbled feta cheese
6 tbsps olive oil
2 tbsps lemon juice
2 tsps chopped fresh oregano
salt and pepper

Cut each tomato into 16 chunks. In a large bowl, combine tomatoes with onion, pepper, cucumber, olives, and cheese in a salad bowl. Mix olive oil, lemon juice, oregano, and seasoning. Pour over the salad and toss lightly to serve.

White Bean Salad

1 lb can cannellini or Great Northern beans, drained and rinsed
1 small onion, finely diced
1 red pepper, deseeded and diced
3 tbsps chopped parsley

1 tsp chopped fresh oregano
8 black olives, halved
grated rind and juice of 1 small lemon
4–6 tbsps olive oil
salt and pepper
2 hard-boiled eggs, quartered

Combine beans, onion, red pepper, parsley, oregano, black olives, and lemon rind. Measure the lemon juice and mix in olive oil to taste. Add seasoning. Toss with the salad and garnish with eggs.

Sandwiches

Avenue Sandwich

Named for Michigan Avenue, a busy street with a mixture of offices and wonderful shops, this is a quick-to-fix sandwich with a sophisticated taste.

8 oz full-fat or low-fat cream cheese, softened	4 leaves of red or green leaf lettuce
8 slices of dark rye bread	1 beefsteak tomato, sliced
celery salt	1 ripe avocado
freshly ground black pepper	lemon juice
2 slices of red onion	

Spread the cream cheese on half of the bread slices. Sprinkle with celery salt and pepper to taste. Separate onion rings and place on top. Add lettuce leaves and tomato slices. Sprinkle again with celery salt and pepper. Peel and slice the avocado and sprinkle with lemon juice. Place on top of the tomato and top with remaining bread. Cut in half and serve immediately with tortilla chips.

Walnut Room Sandwich

This sandwich takes its name from the Walnut Room, an elegant and tranquil restaurant tucked away in the upper reaches of Marshall Field, Chicago's most famous department store.

½ cup mayonnaise	4 slices of Swiss cheese
2 tsps chilli sauce	2 slices beefsteak tomato
1 tsp mustard	4 oz sliced roast ham

2 slices light rye bread	half a small head iceberg lettuce
1 hard-boiled egg, finely chopped	

(makes 2)

Combine mayonnaise, chilli sauce, and mustard. Spread bread lightly with some of this dressing. Add egg to the remainder and enough water to make a thick coating mixture. Layer each bread slice with 2 slices of cheese, 1 tomato slice, and 2 oz of ham. Cut the lettuce in half and place a wedge on each sandwich. Coat each sandwich with dressing and serve immediately.

Pasta with Three Tomatoes

A colorful dish made with fresh red and yellow tomatoes and sun-dried tomatoes tossed with egg and spinach fettucine.

---

1 tbsp olive oil	salt and pepper
1 clove garlic, crushed	pinch of sugar
1 cup sun-dried tomatoes	$1/2$ cup water
$1/2$ tsp chopped basil	1 cup yellow cherry tomatoes
$1/2$ tsp chopped oregano	1 cup red cherry tomatoes
pinch of rubbed sage	1 lb egg and spinach
1 tbsp tomato paste	fettucine, cooked
1 cup red wine	grated Parmesan cheese

(serves 4 as first course, 2 as main course)

In a medium skillet heat oil and cook garlic to soften. Cut sun-dried tomatoes in half and add to the pan with herbs, tomato paste, wine, seasoning, sugar, and $1/2$ cup water. Simmer until tomatoes are tender and sauce is well reduced. Cut cherry tomatoes in half and add to the sauce. Heat through. Toss with the hot, cooked pasta and sprinkle with cheese.

Chicken Flautas Meson del Lago

This is reminiscent of a dish served by one of Chicago's best Mexican restaurants, now sadly closed.

4 large chicken breasts or 6 thighs, skinned and boned	**Salsa:**
2 tbsps vegetable oil	1 small green pepper, deseeded and chopped
1 clove of garlic, crushed	1 bunch fresh cilantro
4 tbsps chopped walnuts	2 chilli peppers, deseeded
1/2 tsp ground cumin	salt
1/4 tsp ground cinnamon	2–4 tbsps lime juice
salt and pepper	2–6 tbsps vegetable oil
4 tbsps raisins	1/2 pint sour cream
1/2 cup heavy cream	
8 bought flour tortillas	

Cut chicken into 2-inch pieces. Heat oil in a skillet and cook chicken, garlic, and walnuts for a few minutes, then add spices, salt and pepper. Cook until chicken is tender. Heat oven to 350°F. Add raisins and cream to the chicken and heat thoroughly. Spoon into tortillas and roll up. Place in a lightly oiled baking dish. Cook for about 15 minutes. Meanwhile, blanch green pepper for 5 minutes in boiling water. Drain. Place green pepper, cilantro, chilli peppers, and salt in a food processor or blender and chop finely. Add lime juice and process. With the machine running gradually pour in enough oil to make a thick sauce. To serve, spoon sour

cream over the *flautas* and top with the salsa. Serve with rice and refried beans, or a tossed salad.

Chicken Vesuvio

Almost every Italian restaurant in Chicago serves a version of this classic dish. Most include potatoes, mushrooms, and black olives in the list of ingredients.

---

2 large potatoes, peeled	flour
2 tbsps olive oil	3 lb chicken, jointed
4 cloves of garlic, peeled	I tsp oregano
1/2 lb button mushrooms, quartered	I cup dry white wine
	I cup black olives, pitted
salt and pepper	

Heat oven to 400°F. Cut each potato into 8 pieces. Heat oil in skillet. Add the garlic and mushrooms and sauté until golden. Remove and drain. Add potatoes and sauté 15 minutes, turning often. Remove and drain. Mix salt and pepper with about 1/2 cup of flour and coat the chicken, shaking off the excess. Add a bit more oil, if needed, and brown the chicken, skin side first. Turn and brown the other side, about 15 minutes in all. Place chicken, garlic, mushrooms, and potatoes in an shallow ovenproof baking dish. Sprinkle over the oregano. Deglaze the skillet with the wine. Pour this liquid over the chicken, add olives and cover the dish. Cook for 25 minutes. Uncover and cook a further 15 minutes or until chicken and potatoes are tender and liquid is reduced. Serve with bread and a green salad or vegetable.

Turkey Fricassée Almondine

An unusual combination of sherry-laced creamed turkey with crispy Chinese noodles and toasted almonds.

---

2 lbs breast of turkey, skinned and boned	3 tbsps dry sherry
1 cup chicken or turkey stock	pinch of nutmeg
4 tbsps margarine	1/2 cup cream
1 small onion, finely chopped	2 tsps light soy sauce
2 sticks of celery, thinly sliced	salt and pepper
1 sweet red pepper, diced	5 oz can of crisp chow mein noodles
1/4 lb mushrooms, sliced	1 cup sliced almonds, toasted
4 tbsps all-purpose flour	

Cut turkey into 1-inch pieces and place in a pan with stock. Cover and simmer gently, about 15 to 20 minutes or until completely cooked. Drain and reserve stock. Heat margarine and sauté the vegetables until softened. Stir in flour and gradually add reserved stock. Add sherry and bring to a boil, stirring frequently. When thickened, add nutmeg, cream, soy sauce, and seasoning to taste. Return turkey to the pan and heat through. To serve, spoon the turkey mixture over the chow mein noodles. Sprinkle with toasted almonds and serve with lightly cooked green beans.

Pike with Mustard Sauce

This popular Midwestern fish is even better with a piquant, yet creamy sauce, fragrant with dill.

---

1 small cucumber, peeled and deseeded
1 cup fish stock
$^1/_2$ cup dry white wine
$^1/_2$ cup heavy cream
3 tbsps mild mustard
3 tbsps vegetable oil
2 tbsps unsalted butter
2 lbs pike or other white fish fillets
$^1/_2$ cup all-purpose flour
2 egg yolks
salt and pepper
pinch of sugar
1 tbsp chopped fresh dill

Cut cucumber into $^1/_2$-inch dice. Blanch 2 minutes in boiling water. Refresh under cold water and drain. In a small saucepan, bring the fish stock and wine to a boil. Reduce to $^3/_4$ cup. Add cream and mustard and set aside. Heat the oil in a large skillet and add the butter. Mix the flour with a pinch of salt and pepper. Coat the fish fillets with the flour, shaking off the excess. Sauté the fish in two batches, about 3 minutes per side. Drain and keep warm. Re-heat the sauce thoroughly and in a separate bowl mix a little into the egg yolks. Beat this mixture into the sauce and heat gently, stirring constantly until thickened. Do not allow to boil. Add salt and pepper to taste and a pinch of sugar, if needed. Add cucumber and dill and pour over the fish. Serve with boiled new potatoes.

Buttered Perch

Lightly breaded and sautéed, this is the most popular way of cooking this delicate lake fish.

2/3 cup all-purpose flour
1/3 cup yellow cornmeal or dry breadcrumbs
1/2 tsp paprika
1/4 tsp onion powder
salt and pepper
vegetable oil
1 stick butter
2 lbs lake perch or other mild-tasting white fish fillets
2 eggs, beaten
chopped parsley
lemon wedges

In a medium-size bowl, mix flour, cornmeal or breadcrumbs, paprika, onion powder, and salt and pepper. Heat about 6 tablespoons of oil in a large skillet and when hot, add 2 tablespoons butter. Cut fillets into even sizes. Dip the fish fillets into the beaten eggs, then coat with the flour mixture, shaking off excess. Fry in several batches about 3 to 4 minutes per side. Drain on paper towels and keep warm. If the butter and oil gets too brown, pour it off, wipe out the pan and start with a fresh amount. Heat 1/2 stick remaining butter and pour over the fish to serve. Sprinkle with chopped parsley and serve with lemon wedges.

Chicago Deep-dish Pizza

Now famous everywhere, this pizza was born on the near north side of the city in two restaurants – Pizzerias Uno and Due.

Dough:
3 1/2 cups all-purpose flour
1 envelope rapid-rise yeast
1 tsp salt
2 tsps sugar
4 tbsps margarine
1 cup warm water
Toppings:
15 oz canned plum tomatoes
2 cloves garlic, crushed
2 tbsps tomato paste
2 tsps fresh chopped
oregano or 1 tsp dried
salt and pepper

any or all of the following:
1–3 oz sliced pepperoni
1/2 small green pepper, deseeded
   and sliced
3 or 4 mushrooms, sliced
6 black olives, sliced
1/2 small can anchovies
1/2 small onion, thinly sliced
4–6 oz mozzarella cheese,
   thinly sliced
olive oil

To make the dough, combine 3/4 of the flour with the yeast, salt, sugar, and margarine in a food processor or bowl. Blend until like fine cornmeal. Add water and enough remaining flour to make a soft dough. Knead about 5 minutes on a floured surface. Use a pastry scraper or spatula to help. Try not to add too much extra flour. Press dough into a lightly greased 14-inch round cake pan. The dough should be thinner on the bottom and have a thick edge. Cover and leave about 30 minutes. Drain the tomatoes, reserving the juice. Slice tomatoes and set aside. Mix juice with garlic, tomato paste, oregano, salt and pepper in a small saucepan and cook gently for about 5 minutes, until thickened. Allow to cool.

Heat oven to 450°F. Prick the pizza base all over and bake 4 minutes. Spread the sauce over the dough and top with sliced tomatoes. Arrange as many toppings in whatever amount you like on top of the tomatoes, ending with cheese. Drizzle lightly with olive oil. Bake for 30 to 35 minutes or until cheese and crust edges are golden brown.

Stockyards Inn Steaks

The Chicago stockyards are closed now, and so is the famous Stockyards Inn restaurant. In its heyday, it was a mecca for Chicago beef eaters.

---

¹/₂ cup sour cream	¹/₂ tsp sugar
1 tbsp chopped fresh chives	1 tsp Worcestershire sauce
2 tbsps chopped fresh parsley	1 tbsp vegetable oil
1 tsp chopped fresh savory	4 x 6–8 oz steaks
1 tbsp red wine vinegar	cut 1¹/₂-inch thick
¹/₂ tsp dry mustard	¹/₂ cup beef stock
¹/₂ tsp Beau Monde seasoning or celery salt	

Mix sour cream with herbs, vinegar, mustard, Beau Monde or celery salt, sugar, and Worcestershire sauce. Heat oil in a heavy-based skillet. When very hot put in steaks and press each one firmly against the pan surface. Turn over and press again. Cook 5 minutes per side over moderate heat for rare, 7 to 8 minutes for medium. Remove and set aside, keeping them warm. Pour out excess fat and deglaze the pan with the beef stock. Bring to a boil until reduced by about a third. Whisk in sour cream mixture and

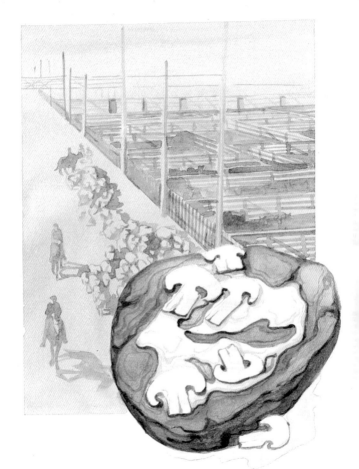

cook over low heat, without boiling, until hot. Pour over the steaks and serve with baked potatoes and sautéed mushrooms.

Sweet Sour Beef

Chicago has many Chinese restaurants. This recipe, remembered from a dinner at a North Shore restaurant, is unusual for a sweet-sour dish.

I cup dried Chinese mushrooms	4 small tomatoes, quartered
I tbsp light soy sauce	¹/₂ cup canned, sliced
2 tsps sesame oil	bamboo shoots
2 tsps rice wine or dry sherry	**Sauce:**
I tsp grated fresh root ginger	I clove garlic, minced
2 lbs sirloin, cut in thin strips	3 tbsps brown sugar
3 tbsps cornstarch	2 tbsps cornstarch
6 tbsps peanut oil	4 tbsps vinegar
I green pepper, deseeded and	I ¹/₂ cups orange juice
cut into I-inch pieces	2 tbsps light soy sauce
3 green onions, cut into	
I-inch pieces	

Soak mushrooms in very hot water for 30 minutes until soft. Drain well. In a large bowl, combine soy sauce, sesame oil, wine or sherry, and ginger and add meat strips. Mix well and marinate 30 minutes. Toss meat strips with cornstarch until well coated. Heat the oil in a wok or large skillet. Brown the meat in two batches. Remove and drain on paper towels. Discard all but I tbsp oil, and add the pepper, onion, and mushrooms. Stir-fry for about 3 minutes. Add tomatoes and bamboo shoots, and stir-fry I minute.

Remove vegetables and drain. Combine sauce ingredients in a small saucepan and cook gently, stirring constantly, until thickened. Return all the ingredients to the sauce and heat thoroughly. Serve with rice.

Kielbasa with Hot Potato Salad

This Polish sausage is still produced by sausage makers in the Chicago area. Here it shares a plate with a German-style potato dish.

2 lbs medium-size waxy potatoes	1/2 cup water
4 strips of bacon, finely diced	1/2 tsp celery or dill seed
1 small onion, finely chopped	1 dill pickle/pickled cucumber,
1 tbsp all-purpose flour	finely diced
1/2 tsp dry mustard	salt and pepper
1 tbsp sugar	2 lbs Kielbasa or smoked sausage
4 tbsps white wine vinegar	

Wash potatoes well and boil in their skins about 20 to 30 minutes or until tender. Drain and peel while still warm. Set aside. In a skillet, fry the bacon until crisp and remove. Sauté the onion until soft. Stir in the flour, mustard, sugar. Whisk in the vinegar and water and add the celery or dill seed. Bring to a boil, stirring constantly. Add more water if very thick. Stir in pickle and season to taste. Cut potatoes into 1-inch pieces and combine with the dressing. Meanwhile, prick the sausage skin all over with a fork. Place it in a large skillet with 1/2 cup water. Cover and simmer gently about 10 minutes. Pour off the liquid and return sausage to the pan. Cook, uncovered, over low heat, turning the sausage frequently until evenly browned. Slice it diagonally into 3-inch pieces and

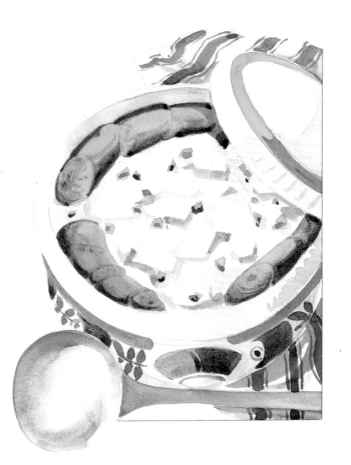

arrange around the potato salad. Serve with bread and sliced tomatoes.

Hickory Smoked Spareribs

The best barbecued spareribs in Chicago are the ones cooked over a hickory wood fire.

4 lb pork spareribs	3 tbsps brown sugar
1 tbsp vegetable oil	1 tsp mustard
1/2 small onion, finely chopped	1 cup tomato ketchup
1 clove of garlic, crushed	salt and pepper
1/2 cup water	hickory wood chips or
1 tbsp Worcestershire sauce	smoke seasoning
4 tbsps vinegar	

Heat oven to 350°F. Place ribs in a large roasting pan. Cover and cook about 1 hour. While ribs cook, start a charcoal fire and prepare sauce. In a small saucepan, heat oil and cook onion and garlic until softened. Add water, Worcestershire sauce, vinegar, brown sugar, mustard, ketchup, and a pinch of salt and pepper. Bring to a boil, then simmer about 15 minutes, stirring frequently. Scatter hickory wood chips over the hot coals. When smoking, place ribs on broiler about 3-inch from the fire. Baste with the barbecue sauce and turn frequently. Broil about 10 to 15 minutes per side. Serve remaining sauce separately.

Note: No hickory wood chips or charcoal fire? Add liquid or powdered smoke seasoning to the sauce and cook ribs under a low broiler for about 15 minutes per side or until tender.

Roast Prime Rib with Chicago Onions

The seasoning for this famous Chicago beef recipe is available ready prepared, but if you make your own, you can add more of the spices you like best.

1 tbsp paprika	4–6 lb forerib/
1 tsp turmeric	standing rib of beef
1 tsp garlic powder	6 medium or 12 small onions
1 tsp celery salt	vegetable oil
1/2 tsp sugar	2 tbsps all-purpose flour
1/4 tsp ground thyme	1/2 cup red wine
1/4 tsp dry mustard powder	1/2 cup beef stock
1/4 tsp cornstarch	salt and pepper
pinch of black pepper	

(serves 6–8)

Heat oven to 375°F. Mix the spices, sugar, cornstarch, and pepper together, adding more of a particular spice, if you like. Rub some of the seasoning mix onto all surfaces of the beef. Reserve the rest. Put beef in a roasting pan and place in the oven. Put unpeeled onions into a pan of water and par-boil for 10 minutes. Place in cold water, then peel, leaving pointed ends untrimmed. Trim root ends. Coat onions lightly with oil and sprinkle with a little seasoning mix. Place around the beef. Roast beef per lb: 25 minutes for rare, 30 to 35 for medium, 40 to 45 for well done. Turn the oven up to 425°F for 15 to 20 minutes before the end of roasting to brown the onions. Remove beef and onions and keep warm. Pour off all but 2 tablespoons of fat and mix in the flour. Brown lightly, scraping the pan often. Pour on wine and stock and bring to a boil, scraping the pan. Cook until thickened, add seasoning and more stock, if too thick. Serve with the sliced beef, onions and mashed potatoes.

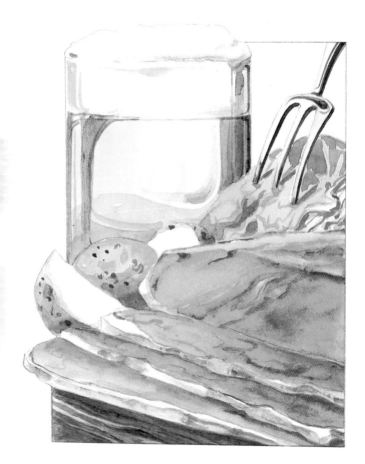

Corned Beef and Cabbage

On St. Patrick's Day in Chicago everyone is Irish, and everyone eats this combination of simmered salt/corned beef, cabbage, and potatoes with spoonful of tangy mustard and warm soda bread.

---

3 lb salt/corned beef brisket
1 tbsp pickling spices
8 large potatoes, peeled and quartered
1 large head of cabbage, core removed
salt and pepper
(serves 6–8)

Place the brisket and spices in a large, deep pan with enough water to cover. Bring to a boil, then simmer about 2 hours, skimming the surface of the liquid as the meat cooks. Add the potatoes and cook about 20 minutes. Cut cabbage into 8 wedges and add to the pot. Cook another 15 to 20 minutes or until vegetables and meat are tender. Remove meat and vegetables from the liquid. Carve the meat into slices and surround with the vegetables.

Pepper Relish

This sweet-sour relish is delicious on a ham, chicken, roast beef or cheese sandwich. Keep several weeks before using it.

---

1 lb each red, green, and yellow peppers, deseeded and finely diced	*1/4 tsp chopped tarragon*
	1/4 tsp ground cloves
	2 tbsps celery seeds

2 small onions, finely diced	³/₄ cup granulated sugar
1¹/₂ tsps salt	3 cups white vinegar
¹/₄ tsp chopped marjoram	
or thyme	

(makes 2 pints)

Place peppers and onions in a large stainless steel pan. Cover with water and bring to a boil. Simmer for 10 minutes and drain. Add herbs, cloves, celery seeds, salt, sugar, and vinegar. Bring to a boil, then lower heat and simmer slowly for 30 minutes or until vegetables are tender and liquid is syrupy. If necessary, boil rapidly, for 5 minutes to reduce liquid, stirring constantly. Ladle into sterilized jars and seal. Store in the refrigerator after opening.

Zucchini Casserole

As a side dish with meat or poultry or as a vegetarian casserole, this versatile mixture is full of warm, sunny flavor.

1 tbsp olive oil	15 oz can chopped plum
1 sweet red pepper, deseeded	tomatoes
and chopped	1 tsp thyme
1 small onion, chopped	salt and pepper
1 clove of garlic, crushed	pinch of sugar
1 cup sliced mushrooms	³/₄ cup grated Cheddar cheese
4 medium-size zucchini, sliced	2 tbsps dry breadcrumbs

In a medium-size pan, heat oil and cook the pepper, onion, garlic, mushrooms, and zucchini about 5 minutes. Add tomatoes, thyme, salt and pepper to taste and a pinch of sugar. Cover and simmer

about 10 minutes. Heat oven to 450°F. Transfer mixture to a casserole dish. Sprinkle the cheese and breadcrumbs over the mixture and bake for 15 minutes. Serve immediately.

Cabbage Rolls

In Polish, these are called Golabki, in Slovak they're Holupki. However you say it, this is one of the most loved dishes from Chicago's eastern European inheritance.

12 cabbage leaves	1 tbsp all-purpose flour
½ cup raw rice	1 lb can chopped tomatoes
1 lb minced beef or pork	½ clove of garlic, crushed
1 onion, chopped	¼ cup chicken stock
salt and pepper	1 tsp chopped thyme
1 egg, beaten	pinch of sugar, salt, and pepper
Sauce:	1 tbsp tomato paste
1 tbsp margarine	chopped parsley

(serves 4–6)

Heat oven to 375°F. Blanch cabbage leaves in boiling water for about 3 minutes, then rinse in cold water. Drain and trim the spines slightly. Cook rice about 10 minutes and drain. In a medium-size bowl, combine rice, onion, meat, seasoning, and enough beaten egg to bind the mixture together well. Divide meat mixture into 12 parts and put a mound on each leaf. Fold up sides and roll up the leaves. Place them close together, seam side down in a casserole. Pour water to come halfway up the rolls, cover and cook for 30 minutes. In a medium-size saucepan melt margarine for the sauce and stir in flour. Add the remaining ingredients except parsley and simmer for 30 minutes. Pour off all but $^1/_2$ cup of liquid from the cabbage rolls and pour over the sauce. Cook uncovered for a further 20 minutes. Sprinkle with chopped parsley and serve.

Blueberry Cheese Cake

Since an abundance of blueberries grows in the Midwest, it seems natural to combine them with a Chicago cheesecake.

I cup zwieback crumbs	I tsp vanilla extract
4 tbsps sugar	2 tbsps all-purpose flour
$^1/_4$ cup melted butter	I lb cream cheese, softened
$^1/_4$ tsp ground cinnamon	I pt blueberries
$^1/_4$ tsp ground nutmeg	4 tbsps sugar
4 eggs, separated	I tbsp cornstarch
I cup sugar	$^1/_2$ tsp lemon juice
I cup sour cream	

(serves 6–8)

Mix together the crumbs, butter, sugar, spices, and press over the bottom and I-inch up the sides of a 9-inch springform pan. Chill until firm. Heat oven to 325°F. Beat egg whites until stiff, then gradually beat in $^1/_4$ cup of sugar. Beat the yolks until thick, then beat in $^3/_4$ cup sugar, sour cream, vanilla, and flour. Gradually beat in the cream cheese until smooth. Fold in the egg whites and spoon into the pan. Bake about I hour or until edges are firm and middle is just set. Cool, then chill for several hours. Combine the remaining ingredients in a small saucepan and simmer until the blueberries thicken. Spread over the top of the cheesecake and chill until firm.

Chocolate Raspberry Tart

A dessert as elegant as North Michigan Avenue. It has an exquisitely rich filling topped with glazed, fresh raspberries.

1 cup all-purpose flour	2/3 cup sugar
pinch of salt	2 eggs
2 tsps sugar	1 egg yolk
1 tbsp cocoa	1/2 tsp vanilla extract
1/3 cup vegetable shortening	1/4 cup light cream
1 tbsp butter	seedless raspberry jam
2 tbsps ice water	1 1/2 cups fresh raspberries
1/2 cup butter	
3/4 cup semi-sweet chocolate chips	

(serves 6–8)

In a medium-size bowl, combine flour, salt, sugar, and cocoa. Work in the fat and butter until mixture is like breadcrumbs. Blend in the water until mixture forms a firm dough. Knead lightly, form into a round and chill. In a medium-size saucepan melt butter and chocolate. Beat in the sugar, eggs and egg yolk, vanilla, cream, and 2 tablespoons raspberry jam. Set oven to 450°F. Roll out pastry and line a 9-inch pie plate or deep flan pan with a false bottom. Prick the base and line with paper. Fill with baking beans and bake blind for 10 minutes. Remove paper and beans. Lower oven to 325°F. Pour chocolate filling in pastry case and bake 35 to 40 minutes or until filling is set. Cool completely, then brush the filling with raspberry jam and top with raspberries. Brush with more jam and leave to set. Serve with whipped cream or ice cream.

Sour Cream Raisin Pie

Rich, satisfying, and very easy. Make your own pastry or use ready-made.

---

pastry for a 9-inch round pie dish
3 eggs
1/2 cup fine granulated sugar
1/4 tsp allspice
1 cup sour cream
1 tsp lemon juice
3/4 cup raisins, roughly chopped
1/2 cup light brown sugar

Heat oven to 450°F. Line pie dish with the pastry, prick the base and fill with paper and baking beans. Bake blind for 10 minutes. Remove paper and beans. Lower oven setting to 300°F. Separate 2 of the eggs and reserve the whites. Mix yolks and remaining whole egg with the granulated sugar, allspice, sour cream, and lemon juice. Cook the mixture gently in a double boiler, stirring constantly until thick. Add the raisins and pour the mixture into the baked pastry. Beat the egg whites until stiff, then gradually beat in the brown sugar to form stiff, glossy peaks. Spread over the filling and bake 15 to 20 minutes. Serve warm or cold.

Cherry Griddle Cakes

These light pancakes with their almond filling make an unusual and delicious dessert.

2 cups all-purpose flour	1/2 cup sliced almonds
2 tbsps baking powder	1/2 cup sugar
1/2 tsp salt	**Sauce:**
2 1/2 cups milk	3 tbsps cornstarch
2 eggs, separated	1 lb can pitted cherries
1/4 cup melted butter	sugar
1 cup almond paste, softened	

In a medium-size bowl combine flour, baking powder, and salt. Gradually add milk, egg yolks, and butter. Mix until smooth. Whisk egg whites until stiff and fold into the mixture. Lightly oil a griddle or large skillet. Pour in about 3/4 cup batter at a time and cook one side of the cakes about 2 minutes or until golden brown. Turn over and cook until risen and set. Spread with almond paste, roll up and place on a baking sheet. Sprinkle cakes with almonds and sugar and broil until browned lightly. To make the sauce, combine the cornstarch, cherries, and their juice in a small saucepan. Cook gently, stirring constantly until thickened. Add sugar to taste and a little water if sauce is too thick. Place pancakes on serving plates and pour the sauce around them. Serve with whipped cream or ice cream, if desired.

Upside-down Apple Cake

My grandmother used to bake her cake in a cast iron skillet, but an ordinary cake pan will do. She served sour cream with it, but whipped cream or ice cream is good, too.

---

^{1}/$_4$ cup butter
^{1}/$_2$ cup light brown sugar
3 tbsps chopped walnuts
2 apples, peeled, cored, and thinly sliced
1^1/$_2$ cups all-purpose flour
1 cup sugar
1^1/$_2$ tsps baking powder
^{1}/$_2$ tsp ground cinnamon
pinch of salt
^{3}/$_4$ cup milk
^{1}/$_3$ cup butter or margarine
1 egg
(serves 6)

Heat oven to 350°F. Melt the butter for the topping in a 9-inch round cake pan or ovenproof skillet. Sprinkle over brown sugar evenly, then walnuts. Arrange sliced apples on top. In a medium-size bowl combine the flour, sugar, baking powder, cinnamon, salt, milk, butter or margarine, and egg and beat for about 30 seconds on a low speed with an electric mixer. Beat 3 minutes on high speed, scraping the bowl frequently. Pour batter evenly over the apple slices and bake for 35 to 45 minutes or until a skewer comes out clean. Turn out onto a large plate, leaving pan over the cake for a few minutes. Serve warm.

Chocomint Pie

Chicago is the candy capital of the Midwest. The local favorite, creamy chocolate mints, also make a lovely, light pie filling.

1½ cups finely crushed chocolate wafers
¼ cup melted butter or margarine
1½ cups milk
1 tbsp gelatine
½ cup sugar
4 eggs, separated
2 oz chocolate mints (not fondant filled)
(serves 6)

Combine crushed wafers and butter or margarine and press into the bottom and sides of a 9-inch round pie dish. Chill until firm. Mix milk, gelatine, sugar, and egg yolks until well blended. Cook gently in a double boiler until custard coats the back of a spoon. Chop the mints and stir into the custard until evenly melted. Put in a bowl and chill until starting to thicken. Whisk egg whites until stiff and fold into the thickening custard. Spoon into the prepared crumb crust and chill until completely set. Serve with whipped cream and top with grated chocolate mints, if desired.

Index

Avenue Sandwich 16

Blueberry Cheese Cake 48
Buttered Perch 28

Cabbage Rolls 47
Cheddar Chowder 7
Cherry Griddle Cakes 55
Chicago Deep-dish Pizza 31
Chicken Flautas Meson
   del Lago 20
Chicken Spaetzle Soup 4
Chicken Vesuvio 23
Chocolate Raspberry Tart 51
Chocomint Pie 59
Corned Beef and Cabbage 43

Dilled Salmon Terrine 11

Greek Salads 15
Greek Taverna Salad 15

Hickory Smoked Spareribs 39

Kielbasa with Hot Potato
   Salad 36

Pasta with Three Tomatoes 19
Pepper Relish 43
Pike with Mustard Sauce 27

Roast Prime Rib with Chicago
   Onions 40

Sandwiches 16
Shrimp de Jonghe 12
Stockyards Inn Steaks 32
Sour Cream Raisin Pie 52
Sweet Sour Beef 35

Turkey Fricassée
   Almondine 24

Upside-down Apple Cake 56

Walnut Room Sandwich 16
White Bean Salad 15
Wild Rice Soup 8

Zucchini Casserole 44